W9-CEY-006

NATIONAL FOOTBALL LEAGUE SUPERSTARS

NFL

by James Preller

SCHOLASTIC INC.

New York   Toronto   London   Auckland   Sydney
Mexico City   New Delhi   Hong Kong   Buenos Aires

COVER PHOTO CREDITS
Bledsoe: Ron Scheffler/NFL Photos. **Shockey:** Joseph V. Labolito/NFL Photos. **S. Rice:** Allen Kee/NFL Photos. **McNabb, Porter:** Al Messerschmidt/NFL Photos. **Holmes:** Greg Trott/NFL Photos.

No part of this publication may be reproduced in whole or in part, or stored in a retrieval system, or transmitted in any form or by any means, electronic, mechanical, photocopying, recording, or otherwise, without written permission of the publisher. For information regarding permission, write to Scholastic Inc., Attention: Permissions Department, 557 Broadway, New York, NY 10012.

ISBN 0-439-53815-7

Copyright © 2003 NFL Properties LLC. Team name/logos are trademarks of the team indicated. All other NFL-related trademarks are trademarks of the National Football League.

Published by Scholastic Inc. All rights reserved. SCHOLASTIC and associated logos are trademarks and/or registered trademarks of Scholastic Inc.

12 11 10 9 8 7 6 5 4 3 2   3 4 5 6 7 8/0

Printed in the U.S.A.
First printing, August 2003
Book design by Michael Malone

NFL Football. It's a team game.

More than any other team sport, football is the most difficult for one person to dominate. Eleven players from each squad take the field at once, twenty-two heavily padded players, trained and prepared for exactly this moment, moving in opposition.

The success of each play depends upon carefully orchestrated movements, precise patterns run by receivers who are shadowed by defensive backs, the cacophonous crash and clash of linemen, grunts and groans, and the crack of pad on pad.

That's the thing: You can't do it alone.

But big players make big plays. Those are the difference makers. The game breakers. The movers and shakers. The best of the best. The sport's superstars.

Let's meet a few of them....

DREW
BLEDSOE

QUARTERBACK
BUFFALO BILLS

BORN: 2/14/72
HEIGHT: 6-5
WEIGHT: 240
COLLEGE: WASHINGTON STATE

[We know we can put **points** on the board.]

THE SAVIOR

And the white knight came riding upon a white steed, his mighty lance glistening in the sun. All the townsfolk cheered and hailed him as a conquering hero…a savior for the franchise…and they called him…Bledsoe.

Okay, sure, maybe it wasn't that bad. But hopes were certainly high, and hearts were surely fluttering, on the day when golden-armed quarterback Drew Bledsoe signed with the Buffalo Bills. They longed to see him stand tall in the pocket, flicking tight spirals with his smooth, easy release. The fans dreamed, more than anything else, of a return to glory. It was a perfect match—because Drew shared those same dreams. For he, too, like the Buffalo franchise, had fallen upon hard times. In 2001 Drew got injured, lost his job as starting QB for the New England Patriots, and couldn't get back on the field. Until the folks at Buffalo came looking for a savior. And Drew answered the call.

DID YOU KNOW?
DREW SHARES THE SAME VALENTINE'S DAY BIRTHDATE AS ANOTHER BUFFALO GREAT, FORMER QUARTERBACK JIM KELLY.

BLEDSOE BY THE NUMBERS
2002 SEASON ▶ COMPLETIONS: 375 • ATTEMPTS: 610 • PASSING YARDS: 4,359 • TOUCHDOWNS: 24 • INTERCEPTIONS: 15 • RATING: 86.0

TOM
BRADY

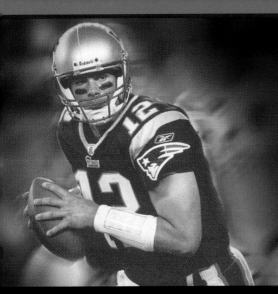

QUARTERBACK
NEW ENGLAND PATRIOTS

BORN: 8/3/77
HEIGHT: 6-4
WEIGHT: 225
COLLEGE: MICHIGAN

[My biggest fear is to end up being a **one-hit wonder.**]

THE REAL DEAL

Everybody knows about Tom Brady and his miracle season, when he seemingly came from nowhere to become Super Bowl MVP. He led the Patriots with confidence and preternatural calm. Nothing fancy, just precision passes and steady leadership. But questions echoed during the off-season: Was it all a fluke? Could this kid truly be for real? Well, Tom Brady heard the questions. He knew about the experts and their nagging doubts. And it fired him up. So Tom went into the 2002 season as if he still had something to prove. And now, at last, that's behind him. The critics have been silenced. Tom has opened their eyes and shut their mouths. Like the NFL's best quarterbacks, Tom is a natural-born leader. In the weight room, on the field, in the classroom, he brings the same intensity to every task. His teammates see it, and they believe in their quarterback. Tom Brady is no flash-in-the-pan. Nope. He's the real deal, and he's here to stay.

DID YOU KNOW?
TOM IS THE YOUNGEST QUARTERBACK TO WIN THE SUPER BOWL, BEATING OUT TWO PRETTY GOOD JOES WHO WERE TIED FOR THE RECORD: MONTANA AND NAMATH.

BRADY BY THE NUMBERS
2002 SEASON ▶ COMPLETIONS: 373 • ATTEMPTS: 601 • PASSING YARDS: 3,764 • TOUCHDOWNS: 28 •
INTERCEPTIONS: 14 • RATING: 85.7

BRETT
FAVRE

QUARTERBACK
GREEN BAY PACKERS

BORN: 10/10/69

HEIGHT: 6-2

WEIGHT: 225

COLLEGE: SOUTHERN MISSISSIPPI

[I couldn't envision myself playing for **another team.**] 4

FOREVER YOUNG

One of the most respected players in the NFL, Brett Favre plays to win. It's the only way Brett knows—and he's been playing, and winning, for a long time now. Add up the numbers, line up the stats, figure the percentages. However you can statistically measure a quarterback, you'll find Brett near the top of all the important NFL quarterback records: total yardage, touchdowns, 300-yard games, whatever. But football isn't math—it's not just numbers on a page. Football is a tough game, best played with heart and soul, aches and courage. What keeps Brett dressing in green and gold every Sunday is his bone-deep competitiveness. He's a Packer, through and through. A man with a childlike passion for the game. The strong-armed Southerner plays with joy and style and heart. Watch him and smile. Brett can still make plays that can make cornerbacks cry.

DID YOU KNOW?
BRETT IS THE ONLY THREE-TIME WINNER OF THE NFL'S MOST VALUABLE PLAYER AWARD (1995, 1996, 1997).

FAVRE BY THE NUMBERS
2002 SEASON ▶ COMPLETIONS: 341 • ATTEMPTS: 551 • PASSING YARDS: 3,658 • TOUCHDOWNS: 27 • INTERCEPTIONS: 16 • RATING: 85.6

MARVIN HARRISON

WIDE RECEIVER
INDIANAPOLIS COLTS

BORN: 8/25/72
HEIGHT: 6-0
WEIGHT: 175
COLLEGE: SYRACUSE

[I live for the **big plays.**]

RECORD BREAKER

Marvin Harrison was the nineteenth player selected in the 1996 NFL Draft. Three wide receivers were chosen before Marvin, and two of them became instant media darlings (Keyshawn Johnson, first pick overall; and Terry Glenn, seventh overall). But, like a well-kept secret, Marvin Harrison quietly went about his job. No tattoos, no jewelry. No flapping lips, no fancy end-zone celebrations. Marvin simply ran his exquisite routes. He caught everything in the air except for influenza. And he brought a commitment to excellence that was second to none. Game after game. Year after year. Until the secret couldn't be kept any longer. Too many records had fallen. Most notably: The most receptions in a single season. More than Herman Moore. More than Jerry Rice. More than anyone. Ever. In the history of the game. Nope, the secret is out. Marvin Harrison is at the top of the list.

DID YOU KNOW?
MARVIN HAS RECORDED 100+ RECEPTIONS IN FOUR CONSECUTIVE SEASONS, EARNING HIM PRO BOWL HONORS EACH TIME.

HARRISON THE NUMBERS
2002 SEASON ▶ RECEPTIONS: 143 • RECEIVING YARDS: 1,722 • YARDS PER CATCH: 12.0 • LONG: 69 • TOUCHDOWNS: 11 • CAREER TOUCHDOWNS: 73

PRIEST
HOLMES

RUNNING BACK
KANSAS CITY CHIEFS

BORN: 10/7/73
HEIGHT: 5-9
WEIGHT: 213
COLLEGE: TEXAS

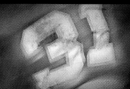

[I hope my story **encourages** other people.]

OFF AND RUNNING

On NFL Draft day in 1997, the experts left Priest Holmes out in the cold. Not a single NFL team selected him. But Priest worked hard and eventually found a job with the Baltimore Ravens. And after four decent years with the Ravens in a limited role (he gained only 588 yards in 2000), Priest signed on as a free agent with the Kansas City Chiefs. The sports world yawned. It was a story of a role player changing teams. No big deal. But in Kansas City, Priest found the perfect situation. His all-purpose talents were ideally suited to coach Dick Vermeil's free-flowing, Rams-style offense. Priest shocked everyone (even coach Vermeil!) by blossoming into a superstar. He led the NFL in rushing yards (1,550) in 2001. What's more, he caught plenty of passes, too—making a case for himself as possibly the best all-around back in the game. Through it all, Priest has remained soft-spoken and modest. But also, heck yeah, proud to have proven the experts so very, very wrong.

DID YOU KNOW? PRIEST LOVES THE MENTAL CHALLENGE OF CHESS, AND PLAYS THE BOARD GAME EVERY CHANCE HE GETS. IN FACT, IN 2002 PRIEST ESTABLISHED A CHESS CLUB AT KANSAS CITY'S POLICE ATHLETIC LEAGUE CENTER.

HOLMES BY THE NUMBERS
2002 SEASON ▶ RUSHING YARDS: 1,615 • YARDS PER CARRY: 5.2 • TOUCHDOWNS: 24 •
RECEPTIONS: 70 • RECEIVING YARDS: 672

DONOVAN
McNABB

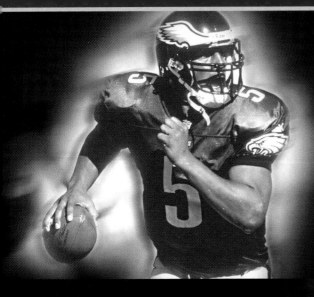

QUARTERBACK
PHILADELPHIA EAGLES

BORN: 11/25/76
HEIGHT: 6-2
WEIGHT: 226
COLLEGE: SYRACUSE

[I play this game to be **the best.**]

NEVER GOING TO REST

In 2001, Donovan McNabb guided the Eagles to their first NFC Championship Game in thirteen years. Unfortunately McNabb and the Eagles fell a little short of their final goal. In 2002, the Eagles again slipped before reaching the finish line, but Donovan McNabb isn't discouraged. He says that he plays to be the best and the only way that he knows to be the best is to work harder than anyone else. And Donovan works hard. During the off-season he spends two weeks a month training at a special camp, participating in punishing exercises and drills. But it's worth it because when Donovan McNabb steps on the field you know that he's there to be the best.

DID YOU KNOW?
BEHIND CLOSED DOORS, DONOVAN DOES GREAT IMPERSONATIONS OF EAGLES HEAD COACH ANDY REID, DEFENSIVE COORDINATOR JIM JOHNSON, AND OTHERS.

MCNABB BY THE NUMBERS
2002 SEASON ▶ COMPLETIONS: 211 • ATTEMPTS: 361 • PASSING YARDS: 2289 • TOUCHDOWNS: 17 • INTERCEPTIONS: 6 • RATING: 86.0

**TERRELL
OWENS**

WIDE RECEIVER
SAN FRANCISCO 49ERS

BORN: 12/7/73
HEIGHT: 6-3
WEIGHT: 226
COLLEGE: TENN-CHATTANOOGA

[I've **got** to be **me.**]

LICENSE TO THRILL

"O" is for Outstanding. Outspoken. Outrageous. Or: the One and Only Owens, Terrell. The wide receiver who can Outrun and Overwhelm the Opposition. Oh, yes. Terrell is all of those things and more. But let's stick with the facts. Terrell is what coaches call a game breaker, a difference maker, a guy who can take over the game and turn the field into his own private playground. Like all big players, Terrell makes big plays. He can catch a short slant pass on the full gallop, juke a couple of defenders, and outrun the rest. Gone, good-bye, it's TD time for T.O.—forward his mail to the nearest end zone. Terrell not only has speed, he has size, too, making him one of the most physical receivers in the NFL. With Owens, the thing to watch is "yards after the catch." That's where he really shines.
Catch him if you can.

DID YOU KNOW? TERRELL SET AN NFL RECORD ON 12/17/2000 WHEN HE MADE 20 RECEPTIONS AGAINST THE CHICAGO BEARS, SHATTERING A 50-YEAR-OLD RECORD SET BY TOM FEARS.

OWENS BY THE NUMBERS
2002 SEASON ▶ RECEPTIONS: 100 • RECEIVING YARDS: 1,300 • YARDS PER CATCH: 13.0 • LONG: 76 • TOUCHDOWNS: 13 • CAREER TOUCHDOWNS: 72

CHAD
PENNINGTON

QUARTERBACK
NEW YORK JETS

BORN: 6/26/76

HEIGHT: 6-3

WEIGHT: 225

COLLEGE: MARSHALL

[Every game is a **learning** experience.]

POISED AND PRECISE

Flashback, October, 2002: The N.Y. Jets had a record of 1-3. They were losing on the field, their offense was struggling, and a promising season was slipping away. So coach Herm Edwards turned to backup Chadwick Pennington and said, "You're in, kid." In response, young Mr. Pennington galvanized the Jets, turned them into believers, and carried them into the playoffs. Extremely smart (he's a coach's son!), Pennington features uncommon poise and uncanny accuracy. He operates the Jets "West Coast" offense like a surgeon—commanding respect in the huddle, reading defenses like dime-store novels, and briskly getting the ball to where it is supposed to be. Nothing fancy, just good decisions and precise throws. He's a natural-born leader. He brought the Jets from the brink of despair and made them division champions, all the while deflecting credit to his teammates. Today, the Jets' future looks bright. And Chad Pennington is reason number one.

DID YOU KNOW?
CHAD WAS THE FIRST QUARTERBACK SELECTED (18TH OVERALL) IN THE 2000 NFL DRAFT.

PENNINGTON BY THE NUMBERS ▶ COMPLETIONS: 275 • ATTEMPTS: 399 • PASSING YARDS: 3,120 • TOUCHDOWNS: 22 •
2002 SEASON   INTERCEPTIONS: 6 • RATING: 104.2

JERRY
RICE

WIDE RECEIVER
OAKLAND RAIDERS

BORN: 10/13/62
HEIGHT: 6-2
WEIGHT: 200
COLLEGE: MISSISSIPPI VALLEY ST.

[The most important thing is to **win.**]

STILL COOKIN'

Jerry Rice is the greatest wide receiver in NFL history. No ifs, ands, or buts. Just check the record book (which, frankly, ought to be retitled, *The Jerry Rice Story*). He's not just a player, he's a full-blown legend. An icon. A Gridiron Great. Jerry holds career records for most receptions, most receiving yards, most touchdowns, most 1,000-yard receiving seasons, most consecutive games with a touchdown, and many more, including most total yards from scrimmage. He's completed an astonishing 18 seasons and shows no signs of slowing down. That's because Jerry just might be the Hardest Working Man in Football. No one trains longer and practices harder. So, you see, it's not just a raw talent thing with Jerry. Talent alone doesn't begin to tell this story. It's about dedication, determination, and drive. It's about wanting to be the best—and then doing all the things necessary to achieve it.

DID YOU KNOW? IN 2000, MEMBERS OF THE HALL OF FAME SELECTION COMMITTEE CHOSE THE ALL-TIME NFL TEAM. AT QUARTERBACK, JOHNNY UNITAS. HE'D BE THROWING TO, OF COURSE, DON HUTSON AND JERRY RICE, WITH JIM BROWN AND WALTER PAYTON IN THE BACKFIELD.

RICE BY THE NUMBERS
2002 SEASON ▶ RECEPTIONS: 92 • RECEIVING YARDS: 1,211 • YARDS PER CATCH: 13.2 • LONG: 75 • TOUCHDOWNS: 7 • CAREER TOUCHDOWNS: 192

SIMEON
RICE

DEFENSIVE END
TAMPA BAY
BUCCANEERS

BORN: 2/24/74

HEIGHT: 6-5

WEIGHT: 268

COLLEGE: ILLINOIS

[I play a let-loose, all-out, **hair-on-fire** style of defense.]

CHAOS THEORY

When you think of the Tampa Bay Buccaneers, you think DEFENSE. Run-stuffing, pass-smothering, quarterback-crushing defense. They've been a top defensive squad for years. But when they signed Simeon Rice after the 2000 season, the Bucs defense really got tough. Simeon's speed-rushing abilities on the outside, combined with Warren Sapp's imposing massiveness on the inside, give Tampa Bay a relentless tandem on the defensive front. After finishing 2001 on fire (11 sacks in his last 9 games), Simeon stepped into the spotlight and proved himself every inch a star. He's part of the new type of tall, extremely fast NFL defensive ends—just what the Bucs needed to contain the likes of athletic quarterbacks like Donovan McNabb and Michael Vick. Simeon has the strength to beat any blocker, and the speed to catch even the fleetest runner. What's that make Simeon? A superstar. The leader of the new breed. And one heck of a headache for the opposition.

DID YOU KNOW? A 1996 FIRST-ROUND DRAFT PICK (THIRD OVERALL) BY ARIZONA, SIMEON QUICKLY FULFILLED LOFTY EXPECTATIONS BY BEING NAMED NFL DEFENSIVE ROOKIE OF THE YEAR AND PRO BOWL ALTERNATE.

RICE BY THE NUMBERS
2002 SEASON ▶ TOTAL TACKLES: 50 • SOLO TACKLES: 43 • ASSISTS: 7 • SACKS: 15.5 • FORCED FUMBLES: 6 • INTERCEPTIONS: 1

JEREMY SHOCKEY

TIGHT END
NEW YORK GIANTS

BORN: 8/18/80

HEIGHT: 6-5

WEIGHT: 252

COLLEGE: MIAMI (FL)

[I'm going to make sure **everybody** knows me.]

RAW EMOTION

Rookies are supposed to be seen, not heard. Their job is to stay in the background, fit in with the team, and to not make waves. Too bad nobody told tight end Jeremy Shockey, who made a big splash when the rookie joined the New York Giants. For starters, Jeremy swaggered into training camp like a proven veteran. But that's Jeremy. He's brash, confident, hard-nosed. He says what he feels, and he does what he likes. He's got speed to beat linebackers on pass patterns, and the brute strength to run over defensive backs (they'd be better off trying to tackle a soda machine). Best of all, young Mr. Shockey plays with raw emotion. A fire that translates into a burning desire to win. That's what fans and teammates recognize in Jeremy— he plays tough—and they love him for it. Already he's one of the finest tight ends in the NFL. Ask him. He'll tell you.

DID YOU KNOW?
IN 2002, JEREMY HAD THE BEST-SELLING ROOKIE JERSEY IN THE NFL.

SHOCKEY BY THE NUMBERS
2002 SEASON ▶ RECEPTIONS: 74 • RECEIVING YARDS: 894 • YARDS PER CATCH: 12.1 • LONG: 30 • NFL SEASONS: 1 • PRO BOWLS: 1

BRIAN
URLACHER

MIDDLE LINEBACKER
CHICAGO BEARS

BORN: 5/25/78

HEIGHT: 6-4

WEIGHT: 254

COLLEGE: NEW MEXICO

I'm honored to carry the **torch** for Bear's **legends** like Butkus, Singletary, and Payton.]

BIG BAD BEAR

Coaches call it "closing gaps." And it works like this: A running back takes the handoff. He sees a hole in the line, opened by two massive offensive linemen. The back accelerates, bursting toward the gap and a long gain. When suddenly—*wham!*—a linebacker steps up to fill the hole. With a crisp hit, he flattens that pesky running back. That's Brian Urlacher for you. He closes gaps as fast as anyone in the NFL. That's partly because Brian has, as they say, "a nose for the ball." But the pure fact is this: Brian is ridiculously fast for a man his size. He single-handedly seems to cover the entire field. Brian can blitz the quarterback, pursue ball carriers sideline to sideline, or drop back twenty yards to provide tough pass coverage. Urlacher runs with the speed of a safety (the position he played in college), but has the mass of a body builder. Urlacher (rhymes with linebacker) is either the NFL's fastest big guy...or its biggest fast guy. Choose your poison. Either way, he's unlike anything the game has seen before.

DID YOU KNOW?
BRIAN HAS BEEN SELECTED TO THE PRO BOWL IN EACH OF HIS THREE NFL SEASONS.

URLACHER BY THE NUMBERS
2002 SEASON ▶ TOTAL TACKLES: 116 • SOLO TACKLES: 97 • ASSISTS: 33 • SACKS: 5.0 • FORCED FUMBLES: 2 • INTERCEPTIONS: 1 • PRO BOWLS: 3

MICHAEL
VICK

QUARTERBACK
ATLANTA FALCONS

BORN: 6/28/80
HEIGHT: 6-0
WEIGHT: 215
COLLEGE: VIRGINIA TECH

[When I pull it down and go, **I'm gone.**]

ELECTRIFYING

Every once in a while an athlete comes along who changes the way his sport is played. You can count these revolutionaries on your fingers: Michael Jordan, Babe Ruth, Bobby Orr, Tiger Woods. Now take a pencil— but don't throw away the eraser—and add Michael Vick to that special list. Yes, he just might be that good. As quarterback for the Falcons, Michael possesses one of the strongest arms in football. But when he tucks in the ball and heads downfield, well, there's never been a quarterback who could do what Michael does. And there's only one word for it: Wow! Now NFL defenses have to try to stop Michael, adapting to his double-threat of pass or run. But remember: Michael played only two years of college ball (where he was 20-1). He's still very young. In 2001, his first year in the NFL, Michael started just two games. He's got a lot to learn. But if he continues to progess at his current pace...WOW!

DID YOU KNOW?

RIFLE ARMS MUST RUN IN THE FAMILY. MICHAEL'S COUSIN
IS NEW ORLEANS SAINTS QUARTERBACK AARON BROOKS!

VICK BY THE NUMBERS
2002 SEASON ▶ COMPLETIONS: 231 • ATTEMPTS: 421 • TOUCHDOWNS: 16 • PASSING YARDS: 2,936 •
RUSHING YARDS: 777 • RATING: 81.6

RICKY
WILLIAMS

RUNNING BACK
MIAMI DOLPHINS

BORN: 5/21/77
HEIGHT: 5-10
WEIGHT: 228
COLLEGE: TEXAS

[I've found a **new home.**]

RUN, RICKY, RUN

Miami coach Dave Wannstedt felt his team was missing something. If the Dolphins were to go deeper in the playoffs, and maybe even reach the Super Bowl, he believed they needed a big, grinding running back. A move-the-chains-type guy who could provide the steady ground game the Dolphins had lacked for years. So they traded for former Heisman Trophy winner Ricky Williams. And Ricky has only done everything they've asked—and more. After three difficult seasons in New Orleans, where he was burdened by sky-high expectations, Ricky was ready for a change. The move to Miami instantly revitalized him. Sure, Ricky is still a punishing inside runner. That will always be at the core of his game. But now he's leaner and faster— routinely getting into the secondary and ripping off long runs. Plus, Ricky is no slouch as a receiver either. He can take short passes and turn them into eye-popping touchdowns. But most important of all, Ricky is smiling. He's happy. Newly confident, relaxed, and ready to roll.

DID YOU KNOW? RICKY WILLIAMS CAN DO IT ALL. IN COLLEGE, HE EARNED ALL-STATE PRAISE AS A LINEBACKER, BUT HE WAS ALSO AN ALL-STATE AND ALL-LEAGUE PICK IN BASEBALL, PLAYING IN THE OUTFIELD. IN ADDITION, RICKY WRESTLED IN THE HEAVYWEIGHT DIVISION AND RAN TRACK, QUALIFYING FOR THE STATE FINALS IN THE 400-METER RELAY.

WILLIAMS BY THE NUMBERS
2002 SEASON ▶ RUSHING YARDS: 1,853 • YARDS PER CARRY: 4.8 • TOUCHDOWNS: 17 • RECEPTIONS: 47 • RECEIVING YARDS: 363

JUST THE FACTS

RUSHING YARDS

Year	Player	Yards
2002	Ricky Williams	1,853
2001	Priest Holmes	1,555
2000	Edgerrin James	1,709
1999	Edgerrin James	1,553
1998	Terrell Davis	2,008
1997	Barry Sanders	2,053
1996	Barry Sanders	1,553
1995	Emmitt Smith	1,773
1994	Barry Sanders	1,883
1993	Emmitt Smith	1,486
1992	Emmitt Smith	1,713
1991	Emmitt Smith	1,563
1990	Barry Sanders	1,304

PASSING YARDS

Year	Player	Yards
2002	Rich Gannon	4,689
2001	Kurt Warner	4,830
2000	Peyton Manning	4,413
1999	Steve Beuerlein	4,436
1998	Brett Favre	4,212
1997	Jeff George	3,917
1996	Mark Brunell	4,367
1995	Brett Favre	4,413
1994	Drew Bledsoe	4,555
1993	John Elway	4,030
1992	Dan Marino	4,116
1991	Warren Moon	4,690
1990	Warren Moon	4,689

PASS RECEIVING YARDS

Year	Player	Yards
2002	Marvin Harrison	1,722
2001	David Boston	1,598
2000	Torry Holt	1,635
1999	Marvin Harrison	1,663
1998	Antonio Freeman	1,424
1997	Rob Moore	1,584
1996	Isaac Bruce	1,338
1995	Jerry Rice	1,848
1994	Jerry Rice	1,499
1993	Jerry Rice	1,503
1992	Sterling Sharpe	1,461
1991	Michael Irvin	1,523
1990	Jerry Rice	1,502

SACKS

Year	Player	Sacks
2002	Jason Taylor	18.5
2001	Michael Strahan	22.5
2000	La'Roi Glover	17.0
1999	Kevin Carter	17.0
1998	Michael Sinclair	16.5
1997	John Randle	15.5
1996	Kevin Greene	14.5
1995	Bryce Paup	17.5
1994	Kevin Greene	14.0
1993	Neil Smith	15.0
1992	Clyde Simmons	19.0
1991	Pat Swilling	17.0
1990	Derrick Thomas	20.0